Short Walks in
The Cotswolds

Guide to 20 easy walks of 3 hours or less

Published by Collins
An imprint of HarperCollins Publishers
77-85 Fulham Palace Road,
Hammersmith, London W6 8JB

www.harpercollins.co.uk

Printed in China

ISBN   978 0 00 735942 4
Imp 002   XJ12502

e-mail: roadcheck@harpercollins.co.uk

Contents

▶ Short walks

Introduction

Walking in the Cotswolds

There are many areas of Britain with individual character but the Cotswolds must stand as one of the most distinctive, with an unmistakable charm and atmosphere all of its own.

This is not remote or wild countryside to walk. However, the Cotswolds has much to offer both the casual and the hardened walker and is best savoured by wandering through the rolling hills and valleys at a gentle pace.

For many visitors, the most memorable impression of the Cotswolds is the mellow stone which seems to bind the countryside together. The Cotswold stone-built houses almost seem to grow out of the landscape, so well do they blend in with the countryside. Its varying hues of yellow, cream, gold and brown are often covered with a frosting of lichen, and inspired J B Priestley to say that the walls know 'the trick of keeping the lost sunlight of centuries glimmering upon them'.

It can seem that the hordes of summer visitors spoil the scenery but, as elsewhere, they tend to concentrate in the well-known 'honey pots', leaving the surrounding countryside to the locals or those 'in the know'. Those out for a quiet stroll will find that there are still many quiet corners, and the walker has a choice of itinerary to suit his or her mood.

Walking is a pastime which can fulfil the needs of everyone. You can adapt it to suit your own preferences and it is one of the healthiest of activities. This guide is for those who just want to walk a few miles. It really doesn't take long to find yourself in some lovely countryside. All the walks are five miles or less so should easily be completed in under three hours. Walking can be anything from an individual pastime to a family stroll, or maybe a group of friends enjoying the fresh air and open spaces of our countryside. There is no need for walking to be competitive and, to get the most from a walk, it shouldn't be regarded simply as a means of covering a given distance in the shortest possible time.

What are the Cotswolds?

The Cotswolds are part of a great belt of limestone that stretches from Lincoln to Dorset. They are often referred to as hills, a misleading and inaccurate term because there is no range of hills as such but rather a plateau of generally medium altitude, most of which lies between 400 and 800ft (120 – 240m). This has been tilted gently to the south-east with the higher, north-western edge forming a distinct and sometimes dramatic boundary.

Elsewhere, the limits of the Cotswolds are more difficult to define. The stone belt continues south into Somerset and Dorset and, to the east, merges gradually into the meadowlands of the Thames. The northern boundary is even harder to determine, and Cotswold country could be said to extend as far as Edgehill.

The western scarp is highest and steepest in its northern and middle sections, reaching over 1,000ft (300m) between Cheltenham and Broadway. In some places it rises 600ft (180m) in less than a mile (1.6km) while the gentle dip slope continues east for up to 20 miles (32km).

At times, the Edge is fairly straight, but elsewhere it has been convoluted by dissecting river valleys, such as around Bath and Stroud. These west-flowing streams have steep gradients, up to 1 in 10, and nearly all flow to the River Severn. The southern end of the Cotswolds lies in the Avon catchment, but by far the largest area is drained by the Thames in the north-east. Here it collects the waters of the longer, more spacious rivers that flow over the dip slope in more or less parallel valleys running north-west to south-east.

View of the Cotswolds from Cleeve Hill

It is evident from detached outliers, such as Bredon Hill, that the limestone once covered a larger area than at present. The scarp slope has receded south-eastwards under the onslaught of erosion that has caused portions of limestone to fall down as the softer rocks underneath have been eaten away.

The distinct, isolated hills now standing in the Severn Vale are mainly the work of streams that have cut back their headwaters into the limestone. Where the stream has been powerful enough, it has isolated the hill from the main plateau. This has already happened to Cam Long Down, Robins Wood Hill, and Churchdown, and will eventually occur at Stinchcombe Hill, where the tongue of land is connected to the main mass by a ridge only a few hundred yards wide.

Another feature of the Cotswolds are the curious dry valleys. These may have been cut when the water table was much higher or by powerful streams of meltwater at the end of the Ice Age when the ground was still frozen.

Geology

The foundations of the Cotswolds were laid down during the Jurassic era some 170 to 100 million years ago when the area lay under the sea and enjoyed a subtropical climate. There was also abundant plant and animal life, so many of the rocks contain fossils.

Although the limestone is the best known of the rocks, it occurs in a series with sands and muds. Very broadly, the clays form the flat plains, the sands form the foothills, and the limestone forms the highest ground.

The limestone is not a uniform rock, varying in colour and composition throughout the area. Geologists have identified two main types, with the older Inferior Oolite underlying the younger Great Oolite.

The Great Oolite once probably overlaid the whole of the Cotswolds, but much of it was eroded away after the area was raised and tilted to the south-east. Consequently, today it is found on the dip slope between about 600 and 800ft (180 – 240m) while the Inferior Oolite covers the highest land above 800ft (240m).

The Inferior Oolite is composed mainly of rounded spheres of calcium carbonate. These so resemble the roe of a fish that the rock has been named from the Greek 'oios lithos' meaning 'egg stone'. It has provided some fine building stone, such as that from the quarry at Leckhampton, but it varies in quality. In places, it consists largely of shell fragments, which has proved good for dry stone walling.

The Great Oolite is a hard white rock that is classed among the finest of building materials. The famous Bath Stone, for example, was used at Blenheim, Eton and Windsor Castle. It was mined from inclined shafts, a convenient method because the stone had to be protected from frost when freshly dug during winter. A maze of storage tunnels surrounded the quarries, and between Box and Corsham, for instance, it is estimated that there are about 60 miles (97km) of underground galleries.

Between the two limestones are layers of fuller's earth and Stonesfield Slate – two more rocks that have played an important part in the history and appearance of the Cotswolds.

Fuller's earth was used for cleansing wool and felting cloth. Stonesfield Slate is a fissile sandy limestone found in the north and mid Cotswolds. It is the traditional tiling material used throughout history since Neolithic times, and forms the characteristic lichen-covered roofs that are features of Cotswold architecture in themselves.

At one time, almost every village had its own quarry. The industry has greatly declined with competition from cheaper materials, however, and very few quarries are now in operation.

Wildlife in the Cotswolds

There are several types of landscape in the Cotswolds, each with its characteristic flora and fauna.

The wolds are good arable land but, apart from fields of growing crops, the walker may well encounter woodland, grassland and rough grazing within the circuit of a single walk.

There are relatively few trees now on the upland, most of the woodland having been cleared by 1200. Beech is the most common species and has been called the 'wood of the oolite'. On shallower soils, ash is more predominant and oak is present on the lower slopes.

Flowers are varied and colourful. In spring, there are banks of wild garlic, their white flowers like exploding cascades of fireworks. There are also bluebells, yellow archangel, wood anemone, primrose and sweet woodruff.

Grassland is found on the highest land at the edge of the plateau, such as at Cleeve Common, with rough grazing on the steepest parts of the scarp. Depending on the level of grazing, there may be wild thyme, rock roses, vetch, cowslips, milkwort, and bird's-foot trefoil. At the sides of the roads look out for travellers' joy, scabious, toadflax, and the characteristic purpley-blue meadow cranesbill. Celandine and marsh marigold may be present in the wetter land of the valley bottoms. Some of the more unusual animals include horseshoe bats in the old quarry workings and large white edible snails in the woodland, said to have been introduced by the Romans. Herds of deer are also quite a common sight.

Woodland Bluebells

Human history

Mesolithic man probably hunted along the scarp after the end of the last Ice Age, preferring the higher, drier ground to the marshy vale below.

These people left few relics but the next wave of settlers gave us lasting memorials. Neolithic farmers crossed the Channel from the Mediterranean around 3500BC, bringing with them their animals and building techniques. These are the people who constructed the long barrows, with a design that was distinctive enough to have been named 'the Severn-Cotswold type'. They were burial places for important individuals and their families, and must have involved considerable organization and effort. At an average of 100 to 200ft (30 – 60m) long and up to 18ft (5.5m) high, they would have taken thousands of man hours to construct as well as thousands of tons of stone – all quarried with antler picks.

Later Beaker immigrants cremated their dead and interred them in round barrows, relatively insignificant structures in comparison. They were followed by the Celtic Iron Age people, who constructed the hillforts along the escarpment. At first, they were built with single ramparts, but later they developed multiple defences, possibly a reaction to the increasing use of the sling. They were highly skilled craftsmen, and the famous bronze enamelled and engraved Birdlip Mirror is among the most prized pieces of Celtic art in Britain.

The Romans invaded the Cotswolds in AD43, meeting little resistance from the local Dobunni tribe. They built the baths at Aqua Sulis (Bath), and Roman Corinium (Cirencester) became second only to London in size and opulence.

Corinium was the provincial capital, at the centre of a web of roads still in modern use – the Fosse Way, Ermin Street, and parts of Akeman Street. The Romans also built villas all over the Cotswolds, choosing sites carefully for their sunny aspects and water supply.

After they withdrew in AD410, the so-called Dark Ages descended, with eventual invasion by the Saxons in AD577. Gloucester and Winchcombe on the Wessex/Mercia border became important centres; indeed, Gloucester was vying to become the national capital.

The most obvious Saxon legacy is the very name of Cotswold itself, for it probably derives from the personal name of 'Cod', a farmer who established himself close to the source of the River Windrush near Winchcombe. The term 'Cotswold' was originally confined to this area but it has gradually encompassed more of the wolds to its present extent.

Wool had been produced in the Cotswolds since Roman times, but it came to full prominence after the Norman Conquest. By the 13th century, it had become immensely important to the national economy. The large local breed of sheep called 'Cotswold lions' produced fleeces up to two stones (12.6kg) in weight which, at first, were exported raw to Europe. Later, Flemish weavers helped to establish a cloth trade and, by the mid 16th century, England was exporting more than 120,000 cloths per year, more than half of which came from the Cotswolds. At the peak of the trade, there were 500,000 sheep in the Cotswolds.

Until the Industrial Revolution in the 18th century, the various processes of cloth production were scattered between the workers' cottages but, with the introduction of machinery such as the power loom, the clothiers gathered all production in one place. Water power was vital and the industry became concentrated alongside the more powerful streams, notably in the Stroud valleys. The supply from the relatively small Cotswold streams proved inadequate, however, and the area lost out to Yorkshire where the rivers are stronger.

Since the advent of the car, the Cotswolds have become much more widely known, and they now form a highly prized residential and tourist centre.

Walking tips & guidance

Safety
As with all other outdoor activities, walking is safe provided a few simple commonsense rules are followed:

- Make sure you are fit enough to complete the walk;

- Always try to let others know where you intend going, especially if you are walking alone;

- Be clothed adequately for the weather and always wear suitable footwear;

- Always allow plenty of time for the walk, especially if it is longer or harder than you have done before;

- Whatever the distance you plan to walk, always allow plenty of daylight hours unless you are absolutely certain of the route;

- If mist or bad weather come on unexpectedly, do not panic but instead try to remember the last certain feature which you have passed (road, farm, wood, etc.). Then work out your route from that point on the map but be sure of your route before continuing;

- Do not dislodge stones on the high edges: there may be climbers or other walkers on the lower crags and slopes;

- Unfortunately, accidents can happen even on the easiest of walks. If this should be the case and you need the help of others, make sure that the injured person is safe in a place where no further injury is likely to occur. For example, the injured person should not be left on a steep hillside or in danger from falling rocks. If you have a mobile phone and there is a signal, call for assistance. If, however, you are unable to contact help by mobile and you cannot leave anyone with the injured person, and even if they are conscious, try to leave a written note explaining their injuries and whatever you have done in the way of first aid treatment. Make sure you know exactly where you left them and then go to find assistance. Make your way to a telephone, dial 999 and ask for the police or mountain rescue. Unless the accident has happened within easy access of a road, it is the responsibility of the police to arrange evacuation. Always give accurate directions on how to find the casualty and, if possible, give an indication of the injuries involved;

- When walking in open country, learn to keep an eye on the immediate foreground while you admire the scenery or plan the route ahead. This may sound difficult but will enhance your walking experience;

- It's best to walk at a steady pace, always on the flat of the feet as this is less tiring. Try not to walk directly up or downhill. A zigzag route is a more comfortable way of negotiating a slope. Running directly downhill is a major cause of erosion on popular hillsides;

- When walking along a country road, walk on the right, facing the traffic. The exception to this rule is, when approaching a blind bend, the walker should cross over to the left and so have a clear view and also be seen in both directions;

- Finally, always park your car where it will not cause inconvenience to other road users or prevent a farmer from gaining access to his fields. Take any valuables with you or lock them out of sight in the car.

Equipment

Equipment, including clothing, footwear and rucksacks, is essentially a personal thing and depends on several factors, such as the type of activity planned, the time of year, and weather likely to be encountered.

All too often, a novice walker will spend money on a fashionable jacket but will skimp when it comes to buying footwear or a comfortable rucksack. Blistered and tired feet quickly remove all enjoyment from even the most exciting walk and a poorly balanced rucksack will soon feel as though you are carrying a ton of bricks. Well designed equipment is not only more comfortable but, being better made, it is longer lasting.

Clothing should be adequate for the day. In summer, remember to protect your head and neck, which are particularly vulnerable in a strong sun and use sun screen. Wear light woollen socks and lightweight boots or strong shoes. A spare pullover and waterproofs carried in the rucksack should, however, always be there in case you need them.

Winter wear is a much more serious affair. Remember that once the body starts to lose heat, it becomes much less efficient. Jeans are particularly unsuitable for winter wear and can sometimes even be downright dangerous.

Waterproof clothing is an area where it pays to buy the best you can afford. Make sure that the jacket is loose-fitting, windproof and has a generous hood. Waterproof overtrousers will not only offer complete protection in the rain but they are also windproof. Do not be misled by flimsy nylon 'showerproof' items. Remember, too, that garments made from rubberised or plastic material are heavy to carry and wear and they trap body condensation. Your rucksack should have wide, padded carrying straps for comfort.

It is important to wear boots that fit well or shoes with a good moulded sole – blisters can ruin any walk! Woollen socks are much more comfortable than any other fibre. Your clothes should be comfortable and not likely to catch on twigs and bushes.

It is important to carry a compass, preferably one of the 'Silva' type as well as this guide. A smaller scale map covering a wider area can add to the enjoyment of a walk. Binoculars are not essential but are very useful for spotting distant stiles and give added interest to viewpoints and wildlife. Although none of the walks in this guide venture too far from civilisation, on a hot day even the shortest of walks can lead to dehydration so a bottle of water is advisable.

Finally, a small first aid kit is an invaluable help in coping with cuts and other small injuries.

Public Rights of Way

In 1949, the National Parks and Access to the Countryside Act tidied up the law covering rights of way. Following public consultation, maps were drawn up by the Countryside Authorities of England and Wales to show all the rights of way. Copies of these maps are available for public inspection and are invaluable when trying to resolve doubts over little-used footpaths. Once on the map, the right of way is irrefutable.

Right of way means that anyone may walk freely on a defined footpath or ride a horse or pedal cycle along a public bridleway. No one may interfere with this right and the walker is within his rights if he removes any obstruction along the route, provided that he has not set out purposely with the intention of removing that obstruction. All obstructions should be reported to the local Highways Authority.

In England and Wales rights of way fall into three main categories:

- Public Footpaths – for walkers only;

- Bridleways – for passage on foot, horseback, or bicycle;

- Byways – for all the above and for motorized vehicles

Free access to footpaths and bridleways does mean that certain guidelines should be followed as a courtesy to those who live and work in the area. For example, you should only sit down to picnic where it does not interfere with other walkers or the landowner. All gates must be kept closed to prevent stock from straying and dogs must be kept under close control – usually this is interpreted as meaning that they should be kept on a leash. Motor vehicles must not be driven along a public footpath or bridleway without the landowner's consent.

A farmer can put a docile mature beef bull with a herd of cows or heifers, in a field crossed by a public footpath. Beef bulls such as Herefords (usually brown/red colour) are unlikely to be upset by passers by but dairy bulls, like the black and white Friesian, can be dangerous by nature. It is, therefore, illegal for a farmer to let a dairy bull roam loose in a field open to public access.

The Countryside and Rights of Way Act 2000 (the 'right to roam') allows access on foot to areas of legally defined 'open country' – mountain, moor, downland, heath and registered common land. You will find these areas shaded orange on the maps in this guide. It does not allow freedom to walk anywhere. It also increases protection for Sites of Special Scientific Interest, improves wildlife enforcement legislation and allows better management of Areas of Outstanding Natural Beauty.

The Country Code
The Country Code has been designed not as a set of hard and fast rules, although they do have the backing of the law, but as a statement of commonsense. The code is a gentle reminder of how to behave in the countryside. Walkers should walk with the intention of leaving the place

exactly as it was before they arrived. There is a saying that a good walker 'leaves only footprints and takes only photographs', which really sums up the code perfectly.

Never walk more than two abreast on a footpath as you will erode more ground by causing an unnatural widening of paths. Also try to avoid the spread of trodden ground around a boggy area. Mud soon cleans off boots but plant life is slow to grow back once it has been worn away.

Have respect for everything in the countryside, be it those beautiful flowers found along the way or a farmer's gate which is difficult to close.

Stone walls were built at a time when labour costs were a fraction of those today and the special skills required to build or repair them have almost disappeared. Never climb over or onto stone walls; always use stiles and gates.

Dogs which chase sheep can cause them to lose their lambs and a farmer is within his rights if he shoots a dog which he believes is worrying his stock.

The moors and woodlands are often tinder dry in summer, so take care not to start a fire. A fire caused by something as simple as a discarded cigarette can burn for weeks, once it gets deep down into the underlying peat.

When walking across fields or enclosed land, make sure that you read the map carefully and avoid trespassing. As a rule, the line of a footpath or right of way, even when it is not clearly defined on the ground, can usually be followed by lining up stiles or gates.

Obviously flowers and plants encountered on a walk should not be taken but left for others passing to enjoy. To use the excuse 'I have only taken a few' is futile. If everyone only took a few the countryside would be devastated. If young wild animals are encountered they should be left well alone. For instance, if a fawn or a deer calf is discovered lying still in the grass it would be wrong to assume that it has been abandoned. Mothers hide their offspring while they go away to graze and browse and return to them at feeding time. If the animals are touched it could mean that they will be abandoned as the human scent might deter the mother from returning to her offspring. Similarly with baby birds, who have not yet mastered flight; they may appear to have been abandoned but often are being watched by their parents who might be waiting for a walker to pass on before coming out to give flight lesson two!

What appear to be harmful snakes should not be killed because firstly the 'snake' could be a slow worm, which looks like a snake but is really a harmless legless lizard, and second, even if it were an adder (they are quite common) it will escape if given the opportunity. Adders are part of the pattern of nature and should not be persecuted. They rarely bite unless they are handled; a foolish act, which is not uncommon; or trodden on, which is rare, as the snakes are usually basking in full view and are very quick to escape.

Map reading

Some people find map reading so easy that they can open a map and immediately relate it to the area of countryside in which they are standing. To others, a map is as unintelligible as ancient Greek! A map is an accurate but flat picture of the three-dimensional features of the countryside. Features such as roads, streams, woodland and buildings are relatively easy to identify, either from their shape or position. Heights, on the other hand, can be difficult to interpret from the single dimension of a map. The Ordnance Survey 1:25,000 mapping used in this guide shows the contours at 5 metre intervals. Summits and spot heights are also shown.

The best way to estimate the angle of a slope, as shown on any map, is to remember that if the contour lines come close together then the slope is steep – the closer together the contours the steeper the slope.

Learn the symbols for features shown on the map and, when starting out on a walk, line up the map with one or more features, which are recognisable both from the map and on the ground. In this way, the map will be correctly positioned relative to the terrain. It should then only be necessary to look from the map towards the footpath or objective of your walk and then make for it! This process is also useful for determining your position at any time during the walk.

Let's take the skill of map reading one stage further: sometimes there are no easily recognisable features nearby: there may be the odd clump of trees and a building or two but none of them can be related exactly to the map. This is a frequent occurrence but there is a simple answer to the problem and this is where the use of a compass comes in. Simply place the map on the ground, or other flat surface, with the compass held gently above the map. Turn the map until the edge is parallel to the line of the compass needle, which should point to the top of the map. Lay the compass on the map and adjust the position of both, making sure that the compass needle still points to the top of the map and is parallel to the edge. By this method, the map is orientated in a north-south alignment. To find your position on the map, look out for prominent features and draw imaginary lines from them down on to the map. Your position is where these lines cross. This method of map reading takes a little practice before you can become proficient but it is worth the effort.

How to use this book

This book contains route maps and descriptions for 20 walks, with areas of interest indicated by symbols (see below). For each walk particular points of interest are denoted by a number both in the text and on the map (where the number appears in a circle). In the text the route instructions are prefixed by a capital letter. We recommend that you read the whole description, including the fact box at the start of each walk, before setting out.

Route instruction
denoted by a capital letter in the text

Point of interest
denoted by a number in the text

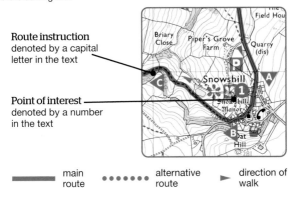

main route ········ alternative route ▶ direction of walk

Key to walk symbols
At the start of each walk there is a series of symbols that indicate particular areas of interest associated with the route.

Birdlife	Other wildlife	Wild flowers
Good views	Historical interest	Woodland
Geology	Literature	

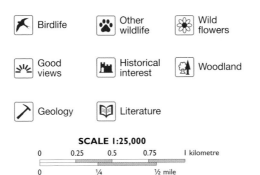

SCALE 1:25,000

0   0.25   0.5   0.75   1 kilometre

0   ¼   ½ mile

Please note the scale for walk maps is 1:25,000 unless otherwise stated
North is always at the top of the page

> 66 The route follows the River Leach to its source at Hampnett and then up onto the wolds before descending once more into the valley with a wonderful view of Northleach 99

The Leach is one of the larger rivers flowing south-eastwards off the wolds. This walk follows the young river for a short way close to its source at Hampnett. The Leach's journey eventually ends with the merging of its waters into the Thames at Lechlade. The route then proceeds up on to the wolds before descending once more into the valley with a wonderful view of Northleach and its church. Although the town is relatively recent – established in the early 13th century – the site itself is an ancient one. An Iron Age track from Chedworth crossed the Leach here and continued on to the camps at Salmonsbury (on the present site of Bourton-on-the-Water) and Maugersbury, at Stow.

The Fosse Way, just to the west of the town, was built by the Romans in about AD60, and was part of a route that stretched from Exeter to Lincoln. Later still, a Saltway was established just to the south, carved by the hooves of pack horses loaded with Droitwich salt en route to London via Lechlade.

Northleach Parish Church of St Peter & St Paul

Northleach & Hampnett

Hampnett

Plan your walk

DISTANCE: 4 miles (6.5km)

TIME: 2 hours

START/END: SP113145 Northleach

TERRAIN: Easy

MAPS:
OS Explorer OL 45;
OS Landranger 163

Route instructions

A Park in the town centre. Head north-westwards along the main street, and continue over the A429 to a gate on the right just past the museum.

1 The parish church of Northleach is one of the three great Cotswold wool churches. There are similarities with the church at Chipping Camden that suggest the work of the same master mason. It is partly 12th century, built on the site of a previous church, but owes much of its 15th century grandeur to the wealth of local wool merchants. The exterior is as notable as the beautifully light and airy interior. Of particular note is the 15th century porch and stone pulpit, and the collection of famous brasses – among the finest in England.

2 The Old Prison, built in 1790 by the prison reformer Sir George Onesiphorus Paul, was a model of its time with exercise yards, baths, and medical care. The historic courtroom is open to the public. The building now houses a rural life collection, including agricultural implements and wagons and is one of the largest publicly-owned regional collections of country life anywhere in the country. The workhouse built at the other end of town led to the saying that Northleach began in prison and ended in the workhouse.

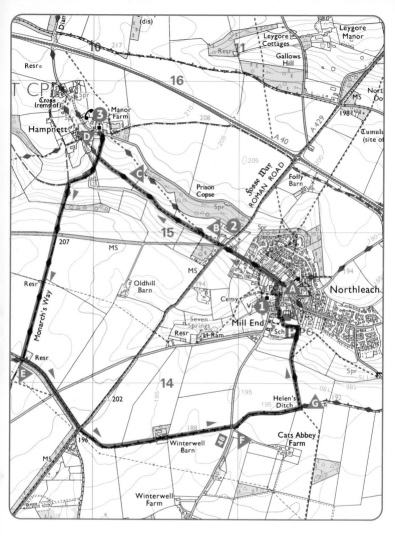

B Go through the gate and bear half-left to the corner. Cross the Leach and turn left to the gate at the end of the field. Pass through the gate, and continue straight on to the next gate.

C Go through the gate and head across the field (it may be under cultivation) aiming just to the right of the big house. Go through another gate and turn right up the track to Hampnett Church.

Northleach & Hampnett

3 The interior of the church was restored in 1868 and it is certainly striking. In the 18th century the rectors were notorious for marrying couples without asking too many questions.

D Leave the church and return down the track. Cross the river and turn left, uphill, at the junction. Pass through a gate halfway up the hill and go straight on at the road. Follow the right-hand field boundaries to the next road.

E Turn left, go straight on at the crossroads and, at the A429, continue straight over the main road onto a path in-between two fields. Follow this path on to a track, passing through farm buildings and on to a tarmac drive to the road.

F Continue ahead along the left-hand dirt track as far as the first gate on the left.

G Turn left through the gate and follow the left-hand field boundary downhill. Continue through another gate, heading straight on keeping the boundary on the left. Go through a further gate, past the tennis courts and cut across the playing field heading towards the church. Join a wall-lined path, then turn right at the end onto a road to return to the town centre.

Hampnett Church

Northleach was once the centre of a large area of sheep production and owes its existence and much of its appearance to the wool trade. It was granted a market in 1227 and, by the 14th century, had become the principal wool market of the central Cotswolds. The Abbey of Gloucester owned the land and planned the town around a triangular market place with 80 plots of land laid out along the north and south sides of the market. Many of these plots have since been combined but can still be seen from high vantage points or detected in the roof lines visible from the market place. The local wool traders became incredibly wealthy, especially those who progressed to become Merchants of the Staple. These were a group of middlemen who held the monopoly of wool export from the Crown and several diverted part of their fortune into the construction of fine buildings including, of course, the magnificent church. Unfortunately, the local industry was tightly controlled by the guilds who proved unable, or unwilling, to adapt to new methods of production and, after the middle of the 16th century, the centre of the trade shifted to Stroud. The Industrial Revolution passed by Northleach and the town has remained relatively untouched for more than two centuries.

❝ Passing through the lovely Cotswold villages of Eastleach Martin and Eastleach Turville this quiet walk follows the winding valley of the River Leach ❞

The River Leach is a tributary of the Thames but in the early part of its course it is seasonal, running above ground only when there is sufficient rainfall. This walk follows a winding valley where the elusive river disappears underground and emerges again beneath deep, weed-covered pools. The countryside here is quiet, offering a chance to escape the crowds and traffic.

The Leach Valley

Keble's Bridge

Route instructions

A Park in Eastleach Turville and walk through the village past the church to the crossroads.

1 This simple stone clapper footbridge is the photographic focal point of the village. It is particularly attractive in spring amid banks of daffodils. It is called Keble's Bridge after the famous local rector, John Keble, who became leader of the Oxford Movement in the Church of England in the early 19th century.

The two villages: Eastleach Turville and Eastleach Martin sit either side of the pretty River Leach with the parish churches of each village only a couple of hundred yards apart linked by the clapper footbridge.

B Turn left along the road to Holwell and continue past the windpump to an iron bargate on the left.

C Pass through the gate and take the path through the meadows close to the river. Go through a gate and follow the river bank to the edge of the woodland ahead, crossing a stile along the way.

D Pass through the smaller, lower gate into the wood and follow the path close to the wall and river on the left. Where the river bears sharp left, carry straight on along the waymarked path.

Plan your walk

DISTANCE: 4½ miles (7.25km)

TIME: 2¼ hours

START/END: SP198052 Eastleach Turville

TERRAIN: Easy

MAPS:
OS Explorer OL 45;
OS Landranger 163

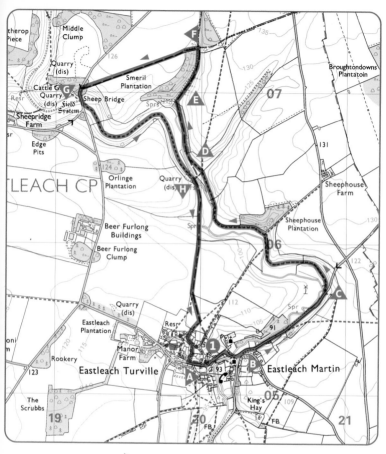

E With the field on your right continue ahead and through woodland until the path is crossed by a well-defined track.

F Turn left on to the track and continue along the left-hand edge of the fields to the road. Turn left and walk a short way almost to the road junction.

G Turn left into the bottom field and follow the valley

bottom round to a gate. Pass through the gate and follow the track to another gate by a bridge.

H Pass though the gate and follow the right-hand field boundaries. At the last field before the houses, bear half-left across the field to a gate and follow the lane back into the village.

The Leach Valley

St Michael and St Martin's Church,
Eastleach Martin

The churches in the two villages are worth taking a look at as you pass through. St Andrew's at Eastleach Turville dates mainly from Norman times with a saddleback style tower roof. St Michael and St Martin's at Eastleach Martin has a 12th century nave and south door but quite a bit of the church was restored during Victorian times.

66 This lovely walk begins and ends at the superb Romano-British villa, follows the wooded banks of the River Coln and then cuts through the ancient Chedworth Woods itself 99

This is a pleasant walk that includes the wooded banks of the River Coln. When planning the walk allow plenty of time to visit the Roman villa, owned by the National Trust, it is regarded as one of the finest examples in Britain. It gives a fascinating insight into 4th century Roman Britain and has some beautiful mosiacs.

Chedworth is an attractive, unspoilt Cotswold village around 600ft (183m) above sea level and extends for almost two miles along the valley of a tributary of the Coln. In the centre of the village is the Parish Church of St Andrew dating from Norman times, although it was substantially rebuilt in the 15th and 16th centuries. The Perpendicular windows lining the nave are unusually large for a church of this size.

Chedworth Woods

Chedworth

Route instructions

1 These are the remains of one of the largest Romano-British villas in Britain. It is thought to have been inhabited as a country house over a period of 250 years. The location was chosen for its sheltered position, water supply, and communications. The first villa was built in the 2nd century but was later altered and enlarged some time in the 4th century, from which the present buildings date. The first remains were discovered by accident in 1864 by a gamekeeper who began to notice fragments of Roman paving and pottery among the rabbit burrows. A museum now houses finds from the site, and there are several impressive mosaics of

varying quality, the remains of two bathhouses and hypocausts for underfloor heating.

The Romans introduced large edible snails to Britain and they can still be seen in and around the villa.

A Use the car park near the villa. Walk back down the road to the gates on the right at the bottom of the hill and turn right along the track. Continue to the road and carry on a short way just past the house on the right.

B Turn right up the steps into the wood. Cross the first track and turn right at a second track. After about

Plan your walk

DISTANCE: 3¼ miles (5.25km)

TIME: 1¾ hours

START/END: SP055134 Car park in Chedworth Woods (East of the Roman Villa remains and North of Chedworth village)

TERRAIN: Easy; one short climb, some mud

MAPS: OS Explorer OL 45; OS Landranger 163

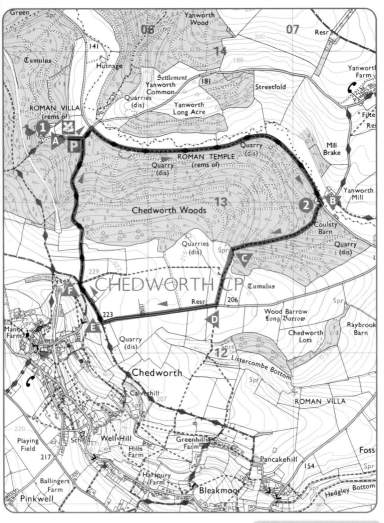

30yds (27m) bear half-left downhill to the main track in the valley. Turn right and follow this track up the valley to the open field.

2 The ancient Chedworth Woods have a great diversity of flora and fauna. Ancient woods are those which were in existence before 1600 and because of this they tend to be very rich in wildlife. Bluebell, primrose and wood spurge can all be seen in the area as well as ramsons (wild garlic) and wild strawberry. There are

Chedworth Woods

also many woodland birds such as tawny owls, woodcock, nuthatch, blackcap, wood warbler and wren. In damp weather the large Roman snail which was introduced by the Romans might be spotted.

C At the entrance to the field, turn slightly left and head uphill across the field, aiming for the marker posts visible in the distance. Bear left slightly as you pass the two trees and join the road.

D Turn right for ½ mile (800m) to a bridleway on the right just as the road starts to descend steeply.

E Turn right and follow the track, passing the buildings on the right and walk through several gates.

F As the track ends continue along the path which bears slightly right, just to the right of the gate straight ahead. Follow the path into the wood and continue downhill. Stay on the path to a stile and then follow the track straight ahead for a short distance. At the road turn left back to the car.

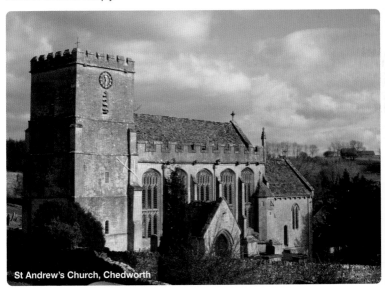

St Andrew's Church, Chedworth

> **"** From Charlton Kings Common there are panoramic views over Cheltenham towards the Malverns and along the Cotswold escarpment as it curves around towards Cleeve Hill - it is worth lingering here to take in the breathtaking view **"**

Above the gorse of Charlton Kings Common there is an unexpected panorama at the top of the hill. Furthermore, as the walk progresses westwards along the edge, the view incorporates new scenery, so allow more time than usual for a walk of this length.

Leckhampton Hill is the site of an Iron Age fort where a defensible area of 6 acres (2.5ha) was enclosed within a single rampart and part of the scarp edge.

Seven Springs & the Devil's Chimney

View from Leckhampton Hill

Plan your walk

Route instructions

A Park in the layby opposite The Seven Springs Inn, off the A436. Turn left on to the A436 and walk up the footpath to the roundabout.

1 It used to be held that the springs issuing from this small hollow below the A436 marked the beginning of the Thames. The Latin inscription reads: *Hic Tuus - O tamesine Pater Septemgeminus fons* ('Here O father Thames is thy sevenfold source').

Although the springs lie at 750ft (228m) – the highest point from which water flows into the Thames – it is now generally acknowledged that the river rises at Thameshead,

3 miles (5km) south-west of Cirencester.

B Turn left, then immediately left again on to the minor road. This is the Cotswold Way, which is clearly waymarked. You will be following this for much of the walk.

C Turn right at the hedge and follow the left-hand field boundary. Continue through the copse, then along the edge of the ridge for about 1 mile (1½km) to a junction of paths atop a rocky step. This area is Charlton Kings Common and is open access land.

2 There is a lot to see in this breathtaking view with Cheltenham spread out

DISTANCE: 4¾ miles (7.5km)

TIME: 2½ hours

START/END: SO966169 Park in the layby opposite the Seven Springs Inn off the A436.

TERRAIN: Easy

MAPS: OS Explorer 179; OS Landranger 163

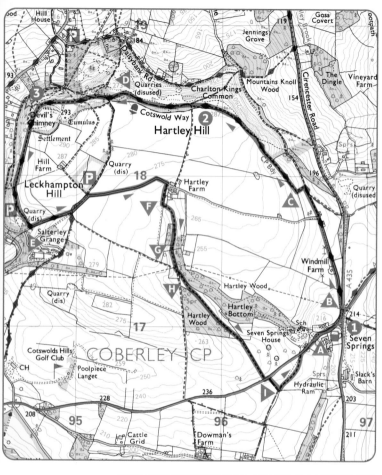

below the scarp. To the right you can follow the escarpment as it curves around to Cleeve Hill which is the highest point in the Cotswolds. Out on the plain ahead rises the distinctive shape of the Malverns, composed of some of the oldest rocks in England and Wales. Further to the west the view includes Gloucester, May Hill in the

Forest of Dean, and the first of the Welsh Hills.

▶ Go straight on and keep to the right of the fence to the triangulation point. With the trig point to your right, continue straight on along the path, until you see a sign pointing downhill to the Devil's Chimney. It's worth making a detour and going down to see this landmark.

Seven Springs & the Devil's Chimney

It's to your right once you've reached the seat on the cliff edge. Head back up to the footpath again then continue southwards along the track, past the quarry to the road.

3 This distinctive, isolated spike of rock is known as the Devil's Chimney and is a popular local landmark. Its exact origin is not known for certain – whether it is the result of differential erosion, a quarryman's joke or a genuine relic of quarrying. Climbing is prohibited to limit erosion.

E Turn left onto the road. You will pass another car park on your left. Turn right into the field immediately before Hartley Farm and follow the wall on the left to a stile.

F Cross the stile and head half-right to the left-hand corner of the plantation. Continue along its edge, with the plantation to your right, to a stile by a pump house.

G Cross the stile and continue ahead with the wood on your left, to the stile on the left just before the corner of the field. Cross this and follow the woodland on the left for about 200yds (180m)

H Cross over to the woodland on the right, carrying straight on at its end to a stile. Cross the stile and carry straight on with the field boundary on your left until you reach the main road.

I Cross the road and turn left, then right on to the footpath on the other side. Follow the path with the field boundary on your left to a stile on the left in the corner of the field. Cross the stile following the right hand field boundary. Cross another stile, continue straight on through a kissing gate to the main road. Turn right for about 100yds (90m) and cross the road to the layby.

Leckhampton Hill was also once the site of intensive quarrying. It lies on the Inferior Oolite, and the freestone here occurs in outcrops up to 138ft (42m) thick. It was already being worked as far back as the reign of Edward III and, during the following centuries, it supplied the material used in the construction of many of Cheltenham's famous buildings. The quarrying reached its peak during the 19th century and, by the late 1800s an extensive system of tramways and railways had been constructed to transport the stone from the rock faces. Some of the inclines were incredibly steep – up to 1 in 2. The trucks were pulled by horses and proceeded down the hill and along 'The Tramroad' north to Cheltenham. A new quarrying concern was set up in 1922 based on optimistic estimates of available yields. After a series of mishaps and local complaints the company was finally wound up in 1925 and quarrying ceased on the hill.

> **This woodland walk is particularly beautiful in spring when the woodland floor is carpeted with bluebells, wild garlic and wood anemones**

This is a varied walk, reflecting both the interesting natural history and the industrial heritage of this valley.

It is here the Thames and Severn Canal enters the Sapperton Tunnel, and the walk follows the old canal and its ruined locks to emerge into the superb ancient woodland of Siccaridge Wood, now a designated Gloucestershire Wildlife Trust nature reserve.

The wood is best seen in spring when it is carpeted in bluebells, wild garlic and wood anemones. Ferns grow in the damp tunnel entrance, and the golden heads of marsh marigolds highlight the course of the canal.

The Golden Valley is one of five valleys converging at Stroud. From Sapperton it continues through Frampton Mansell, Chalford, Brimscombe and on to Stroud.

Sapperton & the Golden Valley

The Daneway

Route instructions

DISTANCE: 3 miles (4.75km)

TIME: 1½ hours

START/END: SO947034 Sapperton

TERRAIN: Moderate; two steep climbs, muddy

MAPS:
OS Explorer 168;
OS Landranger 163

A Park on the roadside just above the church in Sapperton. Return to the junction by the telephone box. Continue ahead and take the public footpath on the right. Cross the minor road and continue to a kissing gate.

B Go through the gate and head half-left downhill, past the large tree to a stile. Cross the tunnel bridge, turn right and follow the canal towpath past the Daneway Inn to the road.

1 This is the western end of a tunnel which at 3817 yards (3481m) long, was the longest in Britain at the time of its completion in 1789. It is part of the Thames and Severn Canal which was built to connect the two rivers between Stroud and Lechlade. The boats were pushed through by men lying on their backs and 'legging' along the tunnel roof. The difficulty of maintaining the water level on the porous limestone, and competition from the Oxford Canal, led to its decline and abandonment early in the 20th century. Work is ongoing to restore much of the Stroudwater and Thames & Severn Canals – most of the route has been designated a conservation area.

C Turn right then immediately left along the footpath marked 'Wysis Way' and walk alongside

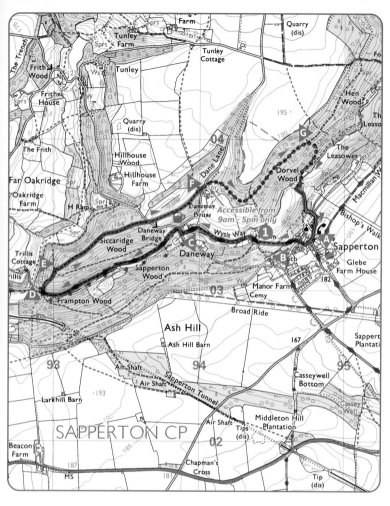

the river to the brick bridge at the western end of the walk.

D Turn right over the bridge and take the middle path uphill through the wood. After 50yds (45m) take a right fork and continue to a junction with another track in a clearing.

Turn left then immediately right and follow the path to the road.

E Go straight across the road and head along the small valley. Ignore the path on the right leading towards the pub. When the path forks, bear right and continue down to the road.

Sapperton & the Golden Valley

View across the Golden Valley

F Turn left then immediately right onto a track and enter the Bathurst Estate (accessible between 8am and 5pm only). Bear right at the fork and follow the main track through the wood. Bear left past a path leading down to a gate and continue as far as a crossing track.

G Turn right downhill, continue over the next track and past a track merging from the left. Take the left fork where the track splits, cross the bridge over the river and then uphill past the house to the road. Turn right and follow the road back to the car.

f Lovely quiet walk following the wooded
valley of the pretty River Frome ™

A lovely quiet walk, following the wooded valley of the pretty
River Frome. This secluded part of the Cotswolds is particularly
pleasant in spring with its abundance of flowers in the woods and
alongside the river.

This upper part of the River Frome is called the Golden Valley,
alluding not only to its autumn colours but also to its general
beauty. Here the river's tiny proportions and secluded banks totally
contrast with its industrial setting just a few miles downstream,
where it once powered the mills of the Stroud cloth industry.

Edgeworth

River Frome

Route instructions

A Park at the top of the minor road signposted 'Church' near the village hall. Follow the road down to a stile on the left just after School House. Cross the stile and head for a gate, go through it, then continue towards the lych-gate by the church.

B Just before the lych-gate, go through the gate on the left and bear half-right down the hill with the fence on your right as far as a gate by a stile.

1 Edgeworth Manor was originally built in the 17th century but was enlarged in the 19th century. It is said to occupy the site of a Roman villa.

C Go over the stile and head downhill turning right at the iron fence. Cross the stream and then walk along the flat valley floor to the footbridge over the River Frome. Head towards the gate by the road. Turn left along the road until it bears sharp left.

D Take the bridleway ahead towards Edgeworth Mill Farm. Bear right following the driveway across in front of the house then take the track on the right alongside the river. Cross the bridge and head straight up the hill then turn left behind the house at the corner of the orchard.

E Follow the bridleway with the fence to your left.

Plan your walk

DISTANCE: 2½ miles (4km)

TIME: 1½ hours

START/END: SO944062 Edgeworth

TERRAIN: Easy

MAPS:
OS Explorer 179;
OS Landranger 163

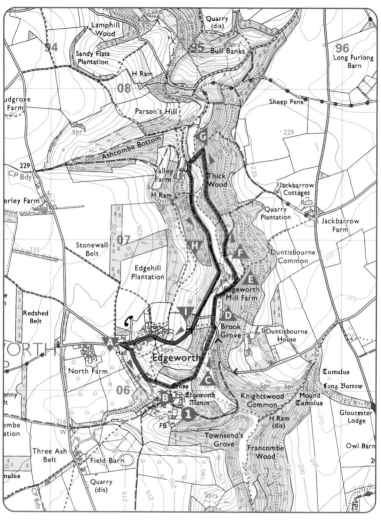

Bear slightly right up towards the wood where there is a waymark.

F Enter the wood and follow the path. Where it forks after about 50 to 60yds (50m) take the left hand path. Follow this path through broken woodland for about ½ mile (800m) as far as a waymarked post.

G At this post you will see a faint path angled back left down towards the river where you will find a footbridge. Cross the bridge

Edgeworth

then bear right then left through the first gate. Cross the field, with the river to your left to a five-bar gate at the far side. Go through the gate and continue across the next field beside the river bearing right to another five-bar gate by Valley Farm driveway.

Valley Farm

Turn left, following the farm drive for about ¼ mile (500m) until it meets the public road.

Turn right up the hill and follow this road back to the car.

66 This walk climbs quite steeply to Fish Hill, it then levels off as you walk along the top of the scarp slope of the Cotswolds towards Broadway Tower where you are rewarded by uninterrupted views over the surrounding countryside **99**

It is quite a steep climb up to Broadway Tower, which at 1024ft (312m) is the second highest point in the Cotswolds, slightly lower than Cleeve Hill at 1083ft (330m), but it is worth the effort as the views from the top are truly superb. From the top of the tower, on a clear day, it is said that you can see 13 counties and the views take in the Black Mountains of Monmouthshire, the Malverns and the Wrekin in Shropshire.

Broadway

View of Broadway

Route instructions

A Use the car park off the B4632 Stratford road. Walk east along the High Street and out of the village for ½ mile (1km) to a public footpath on the left, just after Broadway Waterworks.

B Cross two stiles to pass under the A44. Cross another stile, bear right and continue following the waymarks uphill to the road.

C Take the path opposite into the wood, turning left over the stile. Where the path splits at the top, turn right and, at the next junction, turn left. Follow the path to climb up the steps to the road.

D Cross the road (A44) to follow the Cotswold Way

through the wood to a gate. Continue along the grassy path to the Tower.

1 The Tower occupies the second highest point of the Cotswolds at 1024 feet (312m). The extensive view covers 13 counties and includes the Black Mountains, the Malverns, the Clee Hills, and the Wrekin. It was designed as a folly by James Wyatt and built in 1799 by the Earl of Coventry for his wife. It is 55ft (17m) high, constructed from a non-native stone and remained in private hands until 1972. Since then it has formed the centrepiece for Broadway Tower Country Park. Within the building are exhibitions on the history of the tower and William

Plan your walk

DISTANCE: 3½ miles (5.5km)

TIME: 1¾ hours

START/END: SP100377 Broadway

TERRAIN: Moderate; one long climb, some mud

MAPS:
OS Explorer OL 45;
OS Landranger 150

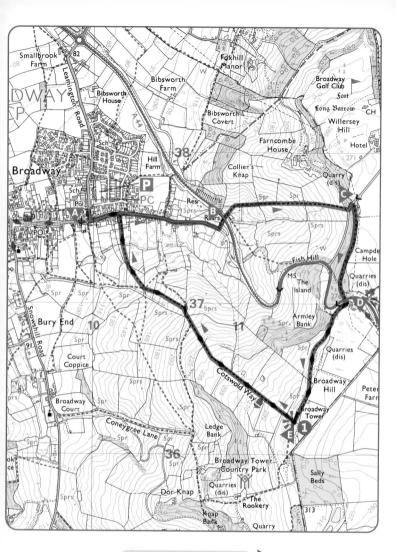

Morris, who used to enjoy holidays at the Tower.

The surrounding country park cover 35 acres (14ha) and includes a red deer enclosure, picnic sites and an adventure playground.

E Turn right down the path beside the fence and follow the signposts back into Broadway.

Broadway

Broadway is named after the width of the main street, dictated by two streams running either side. These are now covered, but the impressive architecture of the buildings, many from the 16th century, can still be seen. Broadway originally prospered from its position on the London to Worcester coach route and, at one time, there were more than 20 inns. The town later became popular as a home for artists and writers. William Morris, in particular, popularized the village when he used to spend holidays at Broadway Tower.

Broadway

> **❝** This lovely 5 mile walk climbs up behind Salter's Hill taking in lovely views over Winchcombe. The route then drops downhill passing close to Sudeley Castle, once home to Henry VIII's 6th wife, Katherine Parr **❞**

Allow plenty of time for this walk to take in the views, perhaps visit the castle, and to wander around Winchcombe, an interesting old town full of character.

Winchcombe nestles below the escarpment, beside the River Isbourne and is an important site with a long history. It rose to prominence as a Saxon town when it became a provincial capital of Mercia.

Sudeley Castle · Winchcombe

Winchcombe & Sudeley Castle

View across Winchcombe

Route instructions

A From Back Lane Car Park walk back to the B4632. Turn left and walk 650yds (600m) to Rushley Lane on the right.

1 The town grew up around the Benedictine Abbey which was founded in AD798 and became one of the largest landowners in the Cotswolds. The Abbey was dissolved in 1539 and there is now no trace of it above ground. St Peter's Church has a splendid weathercock and an interesting collection of 40 gargoyles known as the 'Winchcombe Worthies'.

B Turn right into Rushley Lane and, at the bend, continue ahead up Stancombe Lane to a waymarked gate on the left.

C Follow the waymarks uphill, passing through two more gates. Continue ahead up a steep waymarked path through woodland. Cross the open land at the top to a gate.

D Go through the gate and walk up the left side of the field. At an old wall bear slightly right, cross the stile and continue to the top. Bear left to reach a stone wall. Follow the wall to a stile. Cross the stile and continue down to the next stile.

E Cross the stile and continue down to a gate on the right. Go through and continue to the marker post, then across the next field to the road.

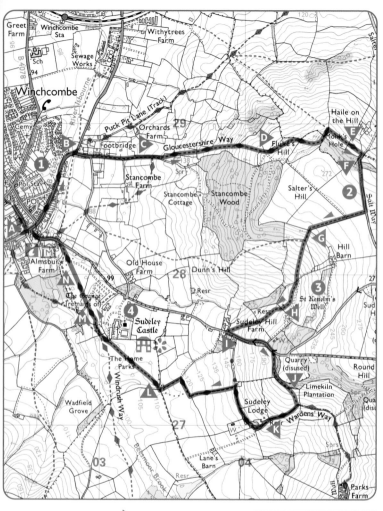

F Turn right for ¼ mile (400m), then turn right along a dirt track to the right of a stone wall. Continue by the wall to a stile in the corner of the field.

2 Salt Way is an ancient route which originated at Droitwich, where the salt was especially pure, and passed through the Cotswolds to London via Lechlade and the Thames.

G Cross the stile and continue to the five-bar gate at the bottom.

Winchcombe & Sudeley Castle

H Follow the track, passing St. Kenelm's Well, to the buildings. Leave the track to bear slightly right across the field to a stile. Head downhill towards the left-hand gate and on to the road.

3 This spring at St Kenelm's Well is said to mark the final halt of the body of Kenelm before it reached Winchcombe. He became King of Mercia as a young boy in AD819 but is believed to have been murdered at the instigation of his jealous sister. The monks at Winchcombe recovered his body and the legend tells that springs gushed out wherever they laid him. The well became a shrine for many pilgrims.

I Turn left uphill to a waymarked path on the right.

J Follow the path in front of the wood and, at a fence, turn left over a stile into the wood. Cross the two stiles at the end and head half-left to the road.

K Turn right and follow the road through the farm. Turn left along a path opposite the next house down to a gate, then turn right. Turn left at the field boundary to the next gate.

L Go through the gate and then over the stile. Head diagonally across the field to the left corner of the castle buildings.

4 Sudeley Castle dates mainly from the 15th century although it was deliberately ruined by Parliamentary forces after the Civil War and even became an inn before restoration between 1837 and 1936. The castle is famous for being home to Katherine Parr, the sixth wife of Henry VIII. She married Sudeley's owner, Lord Admiral Seymour, after the death of the King in 1547 and lived at the castle until her death in 1548. Surrounding the castle are beautiful gardens which were restored and redesigned by Emma Dent in the 19th century and Lady Ashcombe in the 20th century.

M Continue by the fence to a gate on the right. With the play area on the left, walk ahead to a gate by the road.

N Cross the road to the gate ahead. Continue across the field to a gate at the far end and on to the road. Turn left into the town.

> 66 Leaving the lovely village of Stanton this walk climbs up the escarpment to join the Cotswold Way and then drops down through lovely woodland to Stanway where Stanway House is famous for its incredible 300ft (90m) fountain – the tallest in Britain 99

A large section of this walk follows the well-signposted Cotswold Way, visiting two beautiful villages at the foot of the escarpment.

The route climbs over the rough grazing land above Stanton to the top of the escarpment – favoured as a defensive site in the Iron Age – and returns down through some beautiful mixed woodland to Stanway. The last mile or so passes through attractive parkland and fields to Stanton, one of the least spoilt villages in the Cotswolds.

Stanton & Stanway

Stanton

Route instructions

1 Stanton owes much of its restoration to the architect, Sir Philip Stott, who bought the estate in 1906. He spent 30 years restoring the village and, after his death, the council continued in the same manner by constructing houses in the traditional style.

The houses were constructed between the late 16th and mid 17th centuries, some having their dates carved into the lintels – 1604, 1615, 1618. They display all the classic features of the Cotswold style with their drip moulds, stone mullions, and dormer windows.

The church is 12th to 15th century and has strong links with John Wesley the 18th century cleric who preached regularly from Stanton and the surrounding area. Inside there is a rare 14th century wooden pulpit, and the pew ends bear gouge marks made by the ropes attached to the sheepdogs that accompanied shepherds to church.

A Use the car park next to the cricket pitch in Stanton. Turn right out of the car park and, at the junction, turn left and walk as far as the fork near Pear Tree Cottage and the Stott Lantern.

B Turn right and follow the 'Cotswold Way' sign to Shenberrow Hill. Continue on the track and turn right

Plan your walk

DISTANCE: 4¾ miles (7.5km)

TIME: 2½ hours

START/END: SP067342 Stanton

TERRAIN: Moderate; one long climb, some mud

MAPS:
OS Explorer OL 45;
OS Landranger 150

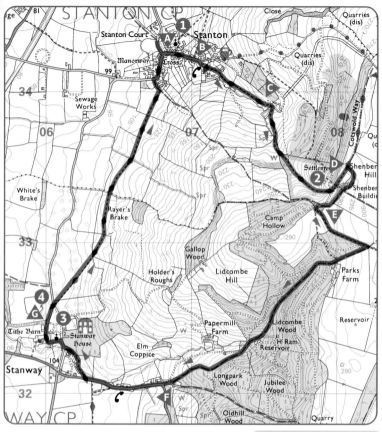

just before a gate down to a stile. Cross this and continue to the next stile.

C Bear right to a stile. Cross this and continue uphill to a stile in the wall on the left. Cross over and head half-right. Follow the waymarks and continue uphill to a gate beside the farm.

2 The hill fort at Shenberrow lies at over 900ft (275m) and commands a good view over the vale. It was built during the Iron Age

some time between 700–150BC although, being of bivallate (double ramparts) structure, it probably dates from the later end of the period. It originally covered about 3 acres (1.25ha), and is one of many hill forts located on the edge of the escarpment.

D Continue ahead to a signpost on the right and turn right, passing through the farm to a gate. Turn right to pass in front of the farm. Continue along the

Stanton & Stanway

right-hand edge of the field, straight on at the first gate and, at the next gate, bear half-left to a stile.

E Turn left and enter the wood ahead. At the junction with the track, turn right and follow the bridleway back into the wood following the marker posts down to the road.

F Turn right and continue along the main road to a stile on the right marked 'Cotswold Way'. Follow the path to the road and turn right past Stanway House to a gate on the right.

3 Stanway House is a fine Jacobean building built by Sir Paul Tracy early in the 17th century. Extensive modifications made in the 19th and 20th centuries were removed in 1948, and much of the present building is original.

Surrounding the house are one of England's finest water gardens, created in the 1720s and since restored. As well as ponds and a formal canal there is the striking 300ft (91m) high single-jet fountain – the tallest in Britain – which was added in 2004.

Past occupants of the house include Dr Thomas Dover. He was known for his mercury-based medicines but is chiefly remembered as the rescuer of Alexander Selkirk – with the literary identity of Robinson Crusoe - from the island of Juan Fernandez in 1708.

4 This rather unusual, thatched, cricket pavilion was given to the village by J.M. Barrie, author of Peter Pan and visitor to Stanway House in the 1920s.

G Go through two gates and follow the waymarks through the parkland and the fields to a gate before the buildings. Turn left to the road and then turn right. At the junction turn left back to the car.

Stanway House

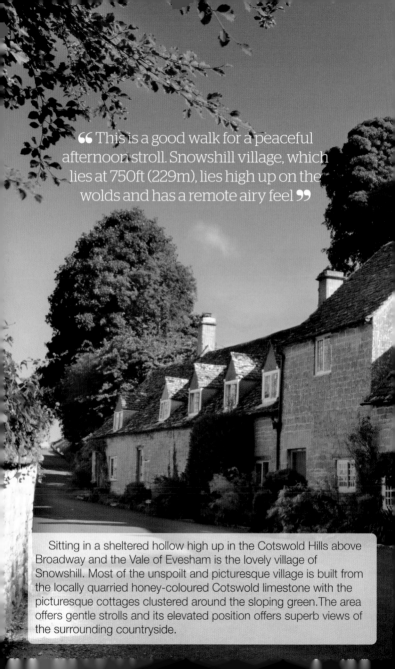

> **❝** This is a good walk for a peaceful afternoon stroll. Snowshill village, which lies at 750ft (229m), lies high up on the wolds and has a remote airy feel **❞**

Sitting in a sheltered hollow high up in the Cotswold Hills above Broadway and the Vale of Evesham is the lovely village of Snowshill. Most of the unspoilt and picturesque village is built from the locally quarried honey-coloured Cotswold limestone with the picturesque cottages clustered around the sloping green. The area offers gentle strolls and its elevated position offers superb views of the surrounding countryside.

Snowshill

Snowshill Manor Gardens

DISTANCE: 4 miles (6.5km)

TIME: 2 hours

START/END: SP096339 Snowshill

TERRAIN: Moderate; one long climb

MAPS:
OS Explorer OL 45;
OS Landranger 150

Route instructions

A Turn right out of the free car park and follow the road past the manor through the village.

1 Snowshill Manor is a popular National Trust property and, in architectural terms, is a good example of a typical 15th to 16th century manor house. The terraced gardens were laid out in 1919 on the basic design of a cottage garden.

The house once belonged to Charles Paget Wade (1919 – 1951), an enigmatic and eccentric architect and antiquary. He acquired not only a West Indian estate but also a very varied collection of items to fill his house – including bicycles, toys, clocks, Japanese armour, farming implements, and musical instruments. He donated these to the National Trust and they are on show inside the house.

B Fork right on to a track. Leave the track at the gate at the bottom of the hill and walk to the left of the fence. Continue alongside the hedge to a stile. Cross the stile and follow the path round to a gate.

C Go through the gate into a large field. Walk up the field heading for the five bar gate at the top.

D Turn right through the gate and take the left fork (Restricted Byway) passing behind the cottages.

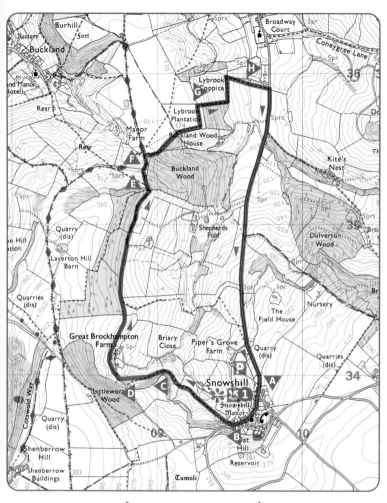

E Continue ahead on the track until you reach a gate. Go through the gate and follow the track downhill to farm buildings.

F Immediately after the farm buildings turn right along a footpath. Cross a stile and continue along a waymarked path.

G Turn right at a fence and walk down the steep hill. Cross a stile and turn left to walk round the edge of a field.

H Cross two stiles, then a third, to join the road. Turn right and follow the road back to Snowshill.

Snowshill

Snowshill Lavender Farm

Snowshill is also the home of Snowshill Lavender. The farm was originally planted in 2000 and now comprises 53 acres, with 250,000 plants and an amazing 70 miles of rows. The free draining limestone soil provides perfect growing conditions for the plants. It is well worth a visit in the early summer when the lavender is in full bloom.

> **❝** This walk climbs steeply up to Uley Bury.
> However, the climb is well worth it
> as the views from the top over the
> Severn Vale are outstanding **❞**

Uley was a much busier place in the 18th century when there were eighteen cloth mills in and around the village. The 'Uley Blue' cloth was used for military uniforms and became as well known as the red cloth of the Stroudwater district.

The site of the Iron Age hill fort at Uley Bury above the village is one of the most spectacular in the Cotswolds and it affords outstanding views over the Severn Vale.

Uley & Owlpen

Uley village

Plan your walk

DISTANCE: 3¾ miles (6km)

TIME: 2 hours

START/END: ST790984 Uley

TERRAIN: Moderate; some steep gradients

MAPS:
OS Explorer 168;
OS Landranger 162

Route instructions

A Park in Uley and walk up the path to the right of the post office. Just before the fields turn right along the signposted footpath between the holly bushes. Turn sharp left just after the start of the stone churchyard wall. Go through the kissing gate and head half-left straight up the hill towards the large tree standing at the edge of the wood. Pick up the well-defined path running along the edge of the wood to a gate.

B Go through the gate and follow the path uphill. The path runs to the left of a metal fence after which there is a metal gate. Head uphill along the edge to the Uley Bury information board.

C Turn left and follow the path to the south-east edge of the hill fort.

1 Uley Bury occupies a superb promontory site with 300ft (90m) drops on all sides except the north. A rampart and ditch provides further protection. It encloses an area of 30 acres (12ha) which is now privately owned arable land, and could have sheltered up to 2000 Iron Age people.

D Turn right between the hillocks and walk downhill through a gate. Keep on the main path steeply downhill, cross a stile and emerge from the woods. Follow the track downhill behind the houses.

walk 11 Uley & Owlpen 57

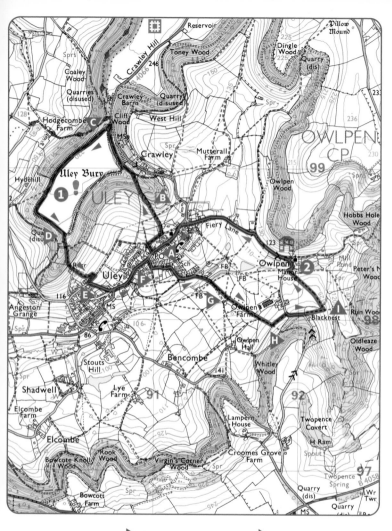

E At the end of the path turn right, go through the metal gate and at the road turn left past Uley brewery to the main road. Turn left and walk as far as South Street.

F Turn right into South Street and follow the road round past the school. Take the right hand fork signposted 'Sheppard's Mill' and leave the metalled road to fork right before the mill and across the stream to a gate.

Uley & Owlpen

G Go through the gate. Continue straight ahead, ignoring the gate and stile on your left and keeping the fence to your left. At the end of the field go through a gate and head in the same direction towards the far left corner of the field to a stile. Head uphill to the next stile just beneath the woods.

H Cross the stile and turn left down to the road. Turn right onto the road for about 100yds (90m) to a gate on the left just before a house. Go through the gate and bear left downhill alongside the fence to a gate on the left.

I Go through the gate and head to the left of the church. Cross the stile onto the track and head down to the road. Turn right and walk along the road back to Uley.

2 The small medieval manor house of Owlpen Manor is noted for its picturesque setting. The building dates mainly from 1450 to 1616 with some 18th century additions. After 100 years of neglect it was restored in Arts and Craft style in 1926 by Norman Jewson. The gardens are open to the public but the house is closed during 2010 for renovation.

Owlpen Manor

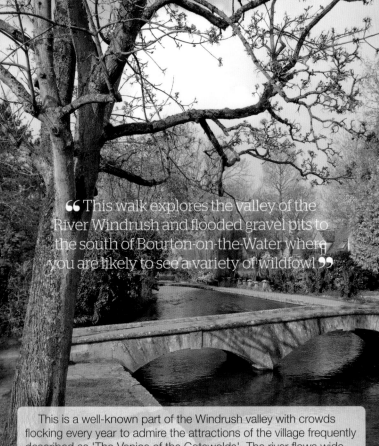

> 66 This walk explores the valley of the River Windrush and flooded gravel pits to the south of Bourton-on-the-Water where you are likely to see a variety of wildfowl 99

This is a well-known part of the Windrush valley with crowds flocking every year to admire the attractions of the village frequently described as 'The Venice of the Cotswolds'. The river flows wide and shallow through the centre, crossed by 18th century low stone bridges, most of which are only wide enough for footpaths.

There are several features of interest in the village but the walk mainly explores the river and valley to the south. The route passes some flooded gravel pits that have become the home for a variety of waterfowl, then ascends the western side of the valley to the small village of Clapton-on-the-Hill, whose church is one of the smallest in the Cotswolds. From here there is a chance to look down into the valley before the gentle descent back into Bourton.

Bourton-on-the-Water

The Model Village, Bourton-on-the-Water

DISTANCE: 3¾ miles (6km)

TIME: 2 hours

START/END: SP170202 Car park beside the main road to the southeast of Bourton-on-the-Water

TERRAIN: Moderate; one climb

MAPS: OS Explorer OL 45; OS Landranger 163

Route instructions

1 Bourton's obvious tourist attractions conceal its importance as an archaeological site, for it has had exceptional historic continuity as a settlement. There is evidence of human habitation since Neolithic times, a period of some 5000 to 6000 years. Just to the east lies Salmonsbury Camp, an Iron Age hillfort that was occupied until Roman times. The Romans crossed the River Windrush here via the Fosse Way, the bridge, of course, having long since decayed.

There are several places of interest in Bourton that the walker may wish to visit before or after the walk.

Here are a few:

- Birdland Park and Gardens is home to over 500 birds including parrots, flamingos, falcons, ibis, pelicans and the only King Penguins in England. The gardens cover 7 acres (2.8ha) of landscaped parks and lakes.

- The Model Village is a replica of Bourton at the time it opened in 1937 at ¹/₉ th scale, complete with authentic stone walled and tiled houses, churches and a miniature River Windrush. It took four years to construct, and follows the detail of the village faithfully, including a model of the model.

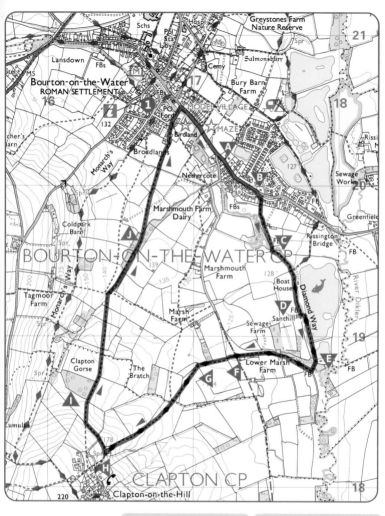

- Bourton Model Railway exhibition covers about 500 square feet (46 sq m) with over 40 British and continental trains travelling through various miniature scenes.

- The Cotswold Motoring Museum opened in 1978 with a 1920s theme but has since expanded to include motoring in the 1960s and 1970s. Among the vintage cars, motorcycles and bicycles are thousands of items of memorabilia, and a collection of over 800 period advertising signs.

Bourton-on-the-Water

A Use the car park beside the main road to the south east of the village. Turn right out of the car park and continue for about ¼ mile (400m) as far as Hilcote Drive on the right.

B Turn right, then first left, and after 40yds (36m) turn right down a public footpath between two houses. Cross the stile at the end and continue ahead through two gates to the footbridge across the river.

C Cross the river and turn left along the edge of a field to a gate. Go through this and the gate ahead to follow the path through the trees. Turn right through a gate into the field and turn left to a gate in front of a barn.

D Turn left over the footbridge, then turn right to the end of the second, smaller lake.

E Turn right, cross the footbridge and stile. Then turn right, following the fence and crossing a stile to reach a gate onto a track.

F Continue straight on through a gate in a gap in the hedge. Walk ahead to the next gate on the left. Go through, turn right and continue to the gate at the edge of the plantation.

G Bear left across the field to the gate ahead and then head slightly left across the next field to the far gate. Cross the footbridge. Continue up the right hand edge of the field to a well-defined crossing track. (Turn left if you wish to visit Clapton-on-the-Hill.)

H Turn right and follow the track to a large field. Bear right across the field following the waymark.

I Continue straight ahead over several fields and waymarked stiles, eventually passing through a plantation to a footbridge on the left.

J Cross over and turn half-right. Cross the next footbridge continuing ahead and over a stile to a track. Continue ahead to a gate and the road. Turn right back into the village.

Bourton-on-the-Water

> 66 The route of the walk takes you up to Dover's Hill, site of the rather eccentric Cotswold 'Olympick' Games. At the end of your walk it is worth taking time to look around Chipping Campden with its fine 15th century church 99

The beautiful curving High Street and imposing church of Chipping Campden are two landmark features of the Cotswolds. Many of the town's buildings date from the time of James I and earlier, while the church is arguably the finest in the Cotswolds. The beautifully preserved state of many of the buildings is largely due to the work of the Campden Trust which was formed in 1929 by a group of local architects and craftsmen. But as well as the town there are other features along the route, including a lovely section of woodland and the viewpoint from Dover's Hill – an incentive for the steep climb from the valley.

A view of Chipping Camden

Chipping Campden & Dover's Hill

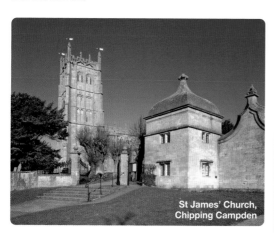

St James' Church, Chipping Campden

Route instructions

1 'Chipping' is found in several Cotswold place names and derives from the Saxon 'ceping' meaning a market. This was to prove very appropriate, for the town later established itself as a market centre for wool.

Woolstaplers Hall was built by a wool merchant in 1340 as a meeting place for the staple merchants to purchase raw fleece. The most famous of the merchants was William Grevel, mentioned by Chaucer in Canterbury Tales. His 14th century house remains almost unaltered in the High Street.

The church of St James was built following his bequest, and is almost entirely 15th century, lending it a unity of style. There are several notable features inside, particularly the brass of Grevel and his wife, among the largest and oldest of Gloucestershire brasses.

Another important local figure was Sir Baptist Hicks, a merchant banker, who built the Market Hall in 1627. He also built the attractive row of almshouses near the church in 1612.

A Park in Chipping Campden. From the main street turn down Back Ends beside St. Catherine's Church towards Hoo Lane. At the sharp right-hand bend, take the first turning on the left into Birdcage

Plan your walk

DISTANCE: 4¼ miles (6.75km)

TIME: 2¼ hours

START/END: SP149390 Chipping Campden

TERRAIN: Moderate; two climbs (one steep), some mud

MAPS:
OS Explorer OL 45;
OS Landranger 151

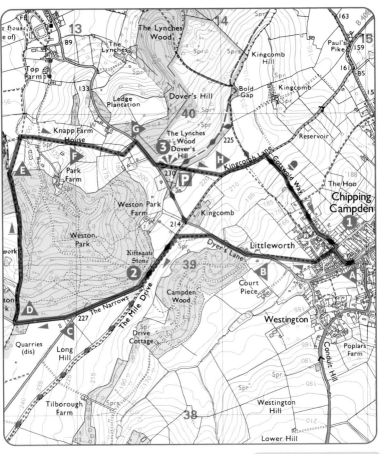

Walk. Continue ahead along the path to a road. Continue over the road to the corner of a field. Take the path half-right uphill to the road.

B Turn right and, after ¼ mile (400m), take the path across the field signposted to Broadway Tower. At the road, turn left and continue to a junction.

2 The Kiftsgate Stone is a holed standing stone on the site of a former 'moot site' where local people discussed business and dispensed justice. The Magna Carta was read from the stone as were the proclamations of monarchs, the last one being that of George III.

C Bear right and continue for ¼ mile (400m) to a bridleway on the right just after a right-hand bend.

Chipping Campden & Dover's Hill

D Turn right and go downhill, keeping close to the right-hand field boundaries when the track emerges from the wood. Re-enter the woodland through a five bar gate and look out for a stile and footbridge when a field comes into view on the right.

E Cross the stile and head half-left across the field. Cross the stile and footbridge near the corner and turn right uphill, crossing a track, to a stile in the top corner of the field.

F Continue in the same direction uphill across two fields and over a stile to a gate. Turn left and join the road through a gate.

G Turn right and, after 300yds (275m), take the path on the left to Dover's Hill. Go straight on over the summit, crossing the stile ahead and continuing across a field to the road.

3 Whitsun Games were probably held on this hill as far back as Saxon times but it was later the site of the famous Cotswold 'Olympick' Games, begun by Robert Dover in 1612.

They were certainly not for the weak in body or spirit, involving such activities as wrestling, hand walking, shinkicking, and a particularly rough pursuit called singlestick fighting. The occasion became very popular and in the 1830s as many as 30,000 people attended.

Unfortunately, the Games became unruly leading to demands for the event to be cancelled. The Games were stopped in 1853.

They were revived in 1951 and now take place on the Friday after Spring Bank Holiday, although not all of the original events are included.

H Turn left and take the second path on the right (the Cotswold Way) back to Chipping Campden.

Chipping Camden

> **❝** This walk is especially beautiful in May when the ancient woodlands are carpeted in bluebells **❞**

There is a lot packed into this relatively short walk with plenty of beautiful scenery to capture your attention. Allow extra time to admire the views and to linger in the lovely woodland, especially in the spring when parts of the wood are carpeted in bluebells.

Standish Wood and Haresfield Beacon stand on westerly facing promontories overlooking the Severn valley. The defensive virtues of the sites appealed to people from very early times, and Randwick Long Barrow, hidden within the wood, is dated at 3000 to 2500BC. There are also three Bronze Age tumuli built around 1000BC and there is the hillfort on Ring Hill constructed during the Iron Age.

Standish Wood is very old, first recorded in 1297 as belonging to Gloucester Abbey. In fact, the whole area used to be much more heavily wooded but it was extensively cleared during World War I. There was a further threat in 1930 from developers but local people managed to raise the funds to buy 327 acres (132ha), which they then gave to the National Trust. The Trust has since planted a mixture of coniferous and deciduous trees and extended its ownership to over 420 acres (170ha).

Haresfield Beacon

Woodland Bluebells

Plan your walk

Worcester
Stratford-upon-Avon
Great Malvern
Evesham
Tewkesbury
Cheltenham
Gloucester
Stroud
Cirencester
Dursley
Swindon
Chippenham
Marlborough
Bath
Devizes

DISTANCE: 4 miles (6.5km)

TIME: 2 hours

START/END: SO832085 Shortwood car park just off the Haresfield road, southeast of the village of Haresfield

TERRAIN: Moderate

MAPS:
OS Explorer 179;
OS Landranger 162

Route instructions

A Use the Shortwood car park just off the Haresfield Road. Walk back towards the road and go through the gap in the wall on the right. Take the leftmost of the three paths, signposted 'Cotswold Way'. Stay on the path until it splits into four. Take the second path on the left and follow it to the road.

B Turn left onto the road and at the next road junction turn left. Cross the road to a stile to the left of Stoneridge Farm. Bear left and cross the field heading towards the stile to the right of the two radio masts.

C Cross the road and turn right. After a few yards cross a stile and head downhill on the path

ignoring crossing paths. Walk down the steep path to the track in the valley (Cotswold Way).

D Turn left onto the track and walk through the wood staying on the track until you meet a road. Turn right and head downhill for ¼ mile (400m) to a bridleway on the left signposted to 'Haresfield Beacon'.

E Follow the path uphill at first, past Cromwell's Stone and on to meet a road. Turn left onto the road and walk 30yds (27m) to a path signposted 'Cotswold Way' on the right.

1 This stone is known locally as Cromwell's Stone, erected to commemorate

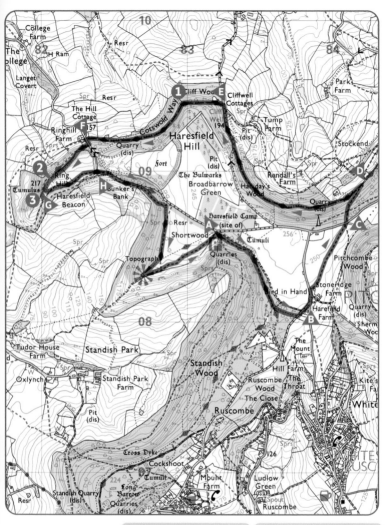

the success of the Parliamentarians in raising the siege of Gloucester in 1643. In July of that year Prince Rupert captured Bristol, leaving Gloucester as an isolated Parliamentarian stronghold in the west of England. King Charles also wanted to open up the River Severn as a supply artery and he surrounded the city on 5th August. It held out for a month, however, until reinforcements arrived under the Earl of Essex – around 15,000 men in all. The King decided it prudent

Haresfield Beacon

to withdraw and gave the Roundheads one of their few successes in the early part of the Civil War.

Why the stone was placed here is not known for certain but, if the trees behind were cleared, there would be an excellent view of Gloucester.

F Turn right onto the path, go through two metal gates and up a steep slope. Cross a stile on the left where the path carries straight on to the right of the fence and bear right towards the triangulation point.

2 The site of the hillfort utilized the natural defences of the promontory. The outlook is excellent with steep slopes on three sides and the fourth closed off by a rampart and ditch across the neck of land to the east. It covers about 16 acres (6.5ha) in all and is so well sited that the Romans made use of it in their military campaigns. Numerous Roman artifacts have been uncovered, including a collection of 3000 coins.

3 From the triangulation point at the end of Ring Hill there is a superb view of the escarpment, and probably the best outlook over the Berkeley Vale.

Several outliers are visible, including Churchdown, Robin Wood's Hill, and Stinchcombe Hill. In the distance is the Forest of Dean, forming a backdrop to the Severn below, and in good conditions it is possible to see the Severn Bridge.

G Turn sharp left and walk along the ridge keeping the valley to your right. Cross the stile and walk along the narrow path with a fence to your left. Pass through a gate and head down towards the road.

H Just before the road turn right down steps and follow the path until it opens out into an open field. Bear half right across the open countryside to the topograph. Turn and head back to the car park.

Haresfield Topograph

66 This short walk circles Ozleworth Manor, the gardens of which are just visible from the footpath 99

This must be one of the quietest parts of the Cotswolds, often with nothing but the farm animals and the wildlife to break the silence. Once enveloped inside the woodland it is hard to imagine that you are barely a mile (1.5km) from the car.

Ozleworth is hardly a village at all, just a few buildings surrounding the 18th century manor house. Indeed, you have to wonder at the presence of the church in such an isolated spot. The present belies the past, however, for the area was once relatively heavily populated.

Marlees Brook valley

Ozleworth

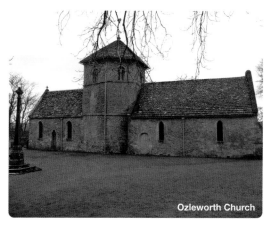

Ozleworth Church

Route instructions

A Park just before the stone gateposts before the sharp bend in the road. Go through the gate signposted 'Church Bridle Path' to the left of the main entrance. At the road turn right and then left at the 'Bridle Path' sign keeping the metal fence on your right.

B Where the road turns sharply to the right, turn left through a gate marked 'Public Bridleway' and then immediately right through a gate into the field. Walk downhill and, at the cottages, turn left heading slightly uphill to a gate at the edge of the wood. Follow the path through the wood alongside the stream to join a track.

1 Incredibly, this row of cottages is the remains of a community once 1600 strong, attracted by the wool industry. The nearby Little Avon River had sufficient strength to power many mills in this area.

2 Glimpses of the 12 acres (5ha) of beautifully restored gardens of Ozleworth Park estate are visible from the footpath. The gardens are privately owned but are occasionally open to the public to reveal vegetable plots, a rose garden, lily ponds, orchard and woodland area.

C Turn left onto the track and then immediately turn right uphill. After about 50yds (45m) go down steps

Plan your walk

DISTANCE: 2 miles (3.25km)

TIME: 1 hour

START/END: ST792934 Ozleworth

TERRAIN: Easy

MAPS:
OS Explorer 168;
OS Landranger 162

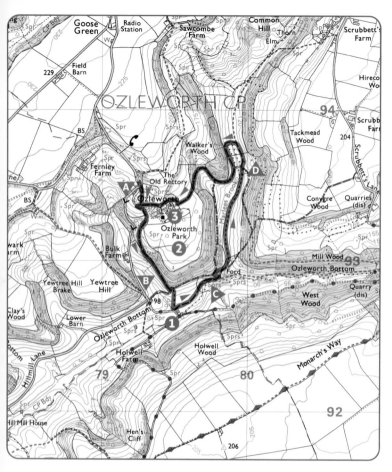

on the right to a footbridge. Cross the bridge, go through a gate and follow the signposted footpath keeping the stream and fence to your left.

D Walk past the old stone bridge to cross the stream a little further upstream on a well-defined track. Walk uphill, along the edge of the wood, across the cattle grid and onto a metalled road.

Just before the gate and stone pillars turn right, signposted 'Bridle Path'. Walk past the pond and turn right onto the road until you meet the outward route at the next 'Bridle Path' sign and make your way back to the car.

3 This small Norman church is remarkable for several features. It stands in a circular church yard,

Ozleworth

Ozleworth Manor

almost 150 feet (45m) in diameter, that clearly exceeded the parish requirements. The church is thought to have been placed in a pre-Christian ritual site.

The most striking feature is probably the unusual six-sided tower, but there is also some superb stone carving on the south doorway and on the west tower arch.

> 66 This walk takes in the village of Castle Coombe, considered by many to be one of the prettiest in the Cotswolds. It also includes some lovely paths alongside the river By Brook 99

Castle Combe is one of the most famous and picturesque villages in the Cotswolds. Centred around the 14th century Market Cross and with attractive rows of cottages, it has been used as a location for several films. The walk passes through the village and also through some lovely woodland and meadow and an interesting side valley.

Castle Combe

Castle Combe Museum

Plan your walk

Worcester
Stratford-upon-Avon
Great Malvern · Evesham
Tewkesbury
Cheltenham
Gloucester
Stroud ·
·Dursley · Cirencester
Swindon
·Chippenham
Marlborough·
·Bath · Devizes

DISTANCE: 4¾ miles (7.5km)

TIME: 2½ hours

START/END: ST845776 Car park West of Upper Castle Combe village and Northeast of Castle Combe village.

TERRAIN: Moderate; some mud

MAPS:
OS Explorer 156;
OS Landranger 173

Route instructions

A Turn right out of the car park onto the road, then right at the next junction. Follow the road down the hill and past the museum. Walk through the village past the Market Cross and across the By Brook. Go past the bridge with the iron gates on the left and continue to the footbridge.

1 The village prospered in medieval times as a centre for the cloth industry with the river By Brook powering cloth mills and cottage weavers producing a red and white cloth called the 'Castlecombe'.

With the decline of the weaving industry the village relied on agriculture,

especially sheep rearing, and its sheep fair attracted flocks from as far afield as Northamptonshire.

A Norman castle to the north-west gave the village its name, but only the earthworks and some stonework now remain.

B Cross the bridge, go over the stile and follow the path along the side of the valley. Keep to the left of the fence for almost ¾ mile (1¼km), crossing an open area and going over two stiles before turning left onto a track.

C Follow the track down to the road junction, turn left and walk to the next road junction. Cross the

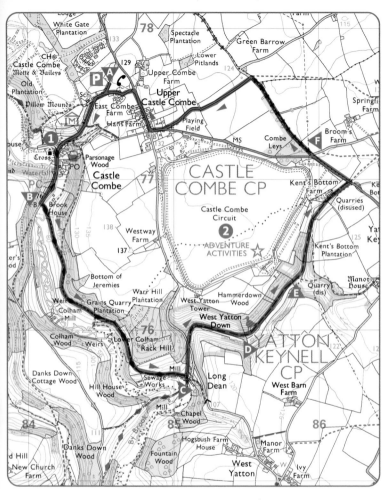

road to the stile just to your left. Cross the stile and turn left to follow the path along the valley bottom, bearing right and climbing a little up to the left to follow the path to a gate.

D Go through the gate and follow the path through woodland to the next gate.

E Go through the gate and carry on straight ahead (do not turn to go up the valley to the right) to go through a gate onto a track. Follow the track to the right of the farm then follow the drive to the road. Follow the road past an entrance to Castle Combe circuit to the junction.

Castle Combe

By Brook, Castle Combe

2 Castle Combe Circuit opened in 1950 on the site of a former World War II airfield and has since been a venue for car and motorcycle race meetings and track days.

F Leave the road and follow the track to the next road. Turn left, follow the road to a junction then turn right through the village. Turn left down the lane by the telephone box, then right at the junction back to the car park.

66 A pleasant walk through gentle Cotswold scenery taking in the villages of Biddestone and Slaughterford where, for part of the route you follow the river By Brook 99

There are no major architectural masterpieces or panoramic views on this route – it is simply a very pleasant walk through small villages and very attractive meadows. Do not be put off by the road section, for the lanes are very quiet.

The large village green and duck pond form the visual centrepiece of Biddestone, a spot that tempts you to linger. Slaughterford was probably named similarly to the other more famous Slaughters, as 'the ford by the sloe trees'.

Biddestone & Slaughterford

The pond at Biddestone

Route instructions

A Park the car in Biddestone. At the road junction by the pond, take the left road signposted to Hartham. Just past the church bear right along Challows Lane and follow the road to the road junction (Weavern Lane) at the bottom of the steep hill.

1 The earliest parts of Biddestone church were completed by the middle of the 12th century. Its most notable feature, however, is the Early English bell turret, the lower section built in the 13th century and the remainder in the 15th.

B Turn right and follow the road above the river to the road junction by the bridge.

Turn right to the sharp right hand bend just ahead.

C Take the footpath ahead passing the old waterwheel after about 200yds (180m) and cross the footbridge. Follow the path through the meadow to the gated weir.

D Cross the weir, go half-left across the meadow and cross a stile in the corner of the field. Follow the path ahead, crossing a stile and over another field to a weir in the corner.

E Cross the footbridge and head for the corner of the field. Cross the stile onto the road and turn right to the White Hart Inn. Turn right between the buildings and across the river. After

Plan your walk

DISTANCE: 4¾ miles (7.5 km)

TIME: 2½ hours

START/END: ST862735 Biddestone

TERRAIN: Moderate

MAPS:
OS Explorer 156;
OS Landranger 173

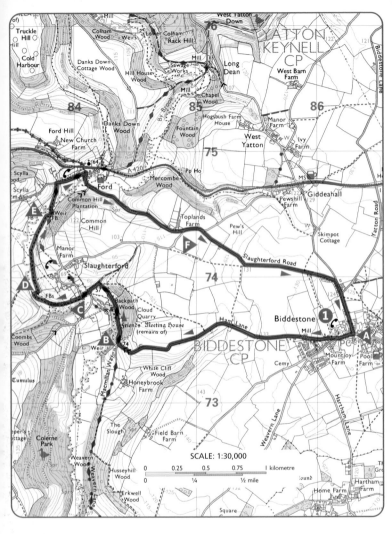

200yds (180m) take the left fork and carry on uphill to a road junction.

F Turn left, then after 300yds (275m), bear right at the next junction. Stay on the road until the next road junction. Turn right and follow the road back to Biddestone.

Biddestone & Slaughterford

The view from Ham Lane

❝ Starting at the Nympsfield Long Barrow the route heads south towards Uley Long Barrow, also known as Hetty Pegler's Tump, and takes in some lovely views over the Severn Vale along the way **❞**

The walk starts from Coaley Peak Picnic Site on Frocester Hill where there are wonderful views over the Severn Vale and a topograph to put names to distant features. On a clear day you can see the Forest of Dean and the Welsh hills beyond. The picnic site and viewpoint are within 12 acres (5ha) of grassland reclaimed from agricultural use in the early 1970s and now seeded with wild flowers.

There are also two important archaeological sites and some lovely woodland to enjoy along the way.

Topograph on Frocester Hill

Frocester Hill & Hetty Pegler's Tump

View from Crawley Lane

Plan your walk

DISTANCE: 4 miles (6.5 km)

TIME: 2 hours

START/END: ST794015 Car park just off the B4066, North of Frocester Hill

TERRAIN: Moderate; one steep climb, some mud

MAPS: OS Explorer 168; OS Landranger 162

Route instructions

A Turn off the B4066 into the 'Nympsfield Long Barrow' car park. Start by walking to Nympsfield Long Barrow 50yds (46m) to the north of the car park. Retrace your steps past the car park following the 'Cotswold Way' marker along the edge to a gate.

1 Nympsfield Long Barrow is an example of the early, true-entranced Cotswold-Severn style of Neolithic chambered tomb, constructed around 2900BC. Unfortunately, it had already been partly destroyed before the first proper excavation in 1862, but at least the lack of a roof offers the chance of examining the general layout.

A short passage from the eastern end leads to three chambers where the remains of 16 skeletons and pottery were found in the 1862 excavation.

The mound was surrounded by a low dry stone wall, most of which is reconstructed. The upright slabs, however, are original.

B Go through the gate (Frocester Hill Viewpoint is a few yards to the right) and follow the path through the quarry, up steps to the road.

C Turn left onto the road and at the next crossroads turn right and then right again signposted 'Cotswold Way'.

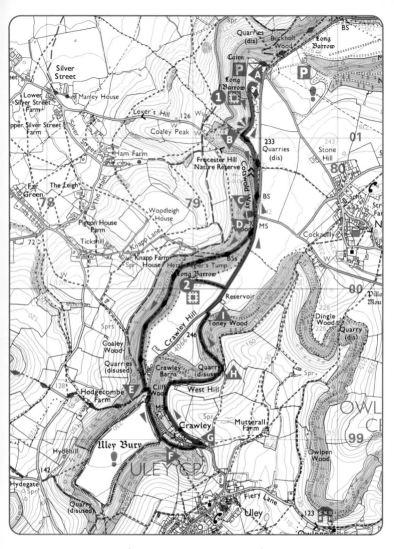

D Follow the path steeply downhill. Take the left fork where the path splits into two, staying on the Cotswold Way for ¾ mile (1.2kms) to a gate near the B4006.

E Go through the gate then turn right through another gate just before the road. At the Uley Bury information board turn left across open countryside to where the path forks after

Frocester Hill & Hetty Pegler's Tump

300yds (275m). Take the left fork downhill.

F After 50yds (46m) turn left through a gate and stay on the bridleway downhill to the road. Turn right onto the road for 50yds (46m).

G Turn left onto Crawley Lane and follow the road heading towards the house which is visible across the valley. Turn right at the barns and take the path to the left of the hedge. Follow the path uphill then slightly downhill to a crossroads in the path.

Hetty Pegler's Tump

H Take the left path uphill and after about 250yds (230m) turn right onto the larger path following it to the main road (B4066).

I Turn right and, if desired, make a detour to 'Uley Long Barrow' (Hetty Pegler's Tump). Carry on along the road to the Frocester/Nympsfield road junction. Turn left down the road to Frocester then right onto the Cotswold Way, retracing your steps back to the car park.

2 Hetty Pegler's Tump (officially Uley Long Barrow), is a fine example of a Neolithic chambered tomb. It was named after Hester Pegler, the wife of the owner of the field in the 17th century. In common with Belas Knap it is of particular interest because it is still roofed. The tomb is virtually intact although some parts have been reconstructed. It is of average size, 120ft (37m) long and 80ft (24m) wide with a 3ft (1m) high entrance capped by a large portal stone. Inside there are two pairs of side chambers off a central passage 22ft (6.5m) long.

For safety reasons there is no access to the interior of the barrow.

The tomb is known to have been opened several times, and 19th century excavations revealed the remains of up to 24 people as well as Roman pottery and a 14th century coin.

The walk begins in Wotton which lies under the escarpment edge. Its full title of 'under-Edge' was added to its Saxon prefix much later, in the 14th century. It came to prominence with the growth of the wool trade, becoming one of the most important wool towns in the Cotswolds. An influx of Flemish weavers gave the industry a boost and, by the early 17th century, the trade was well established, with half the working population involved in some way with the production of cloth.

Serious riots in 1825 were indicative of the decline of the trade in the 19th century, but the town managed to foster other local industries and today houses a thriving community. It also managed to preserve much of its fine architectural heritage, such as the ancient street called The Chipping, with its 16th century timbered houses and 18th century town hall.

In Church Street there is an attractive row of 17th century almshouses while, elsewhere, the elegant 18th century houses of the wealthy merchants flank the streets. There are plenty of other noteworthy buildings in the town for those with an interest in architecture.

Wotton-under-Edge & the Tyndale Monument

View of Wotton-under-Edge

Plan your walk

DISTANCE: 4½ miles (7.25km)

TIME: 2¼ hours

START/END: ST759933 Wotton-under-Edge

TERRAIN: Moderate; muddy in places

MAPS:
OS Explorer 167;
OS Landranger 162

Route instructions

A Use the car park 50yds (46m) down the hill from the monument. Walk back to the monument and continue west up the B4508 to Tabernacle Pitch on the right.

B Turn right and follow the road around to the left. At the end of the road continue up a steep path to the road. Turn right along the road to the top of the hill and a footpath signposted 'Public Bridleway' on the left.

C Follow the footpath towards the trees, joining the Cotswold Way along the edge of the woodland.

D Stay on the Cotswold Way past a well-defined path to the right (the inward route) and take two right-hand forks past the fort to a 'T' junction. Turn right to a complex of paths.

1 The Iron Age ditches and ramparts of the hillfort of Brackenbury Ditches enclose a roughly triangular area of 6 acres (2.5ha), protected on two sides by the scarp slope and a double ditch and rampart on the third side at the neck. The outer ditch has been cleared but most of the site is overgrown and has never been excavated.

E Turn left through the gate, emerge from the trees and continue to the monument. Carry on downhill past the monument down the steep steps to the bottom.

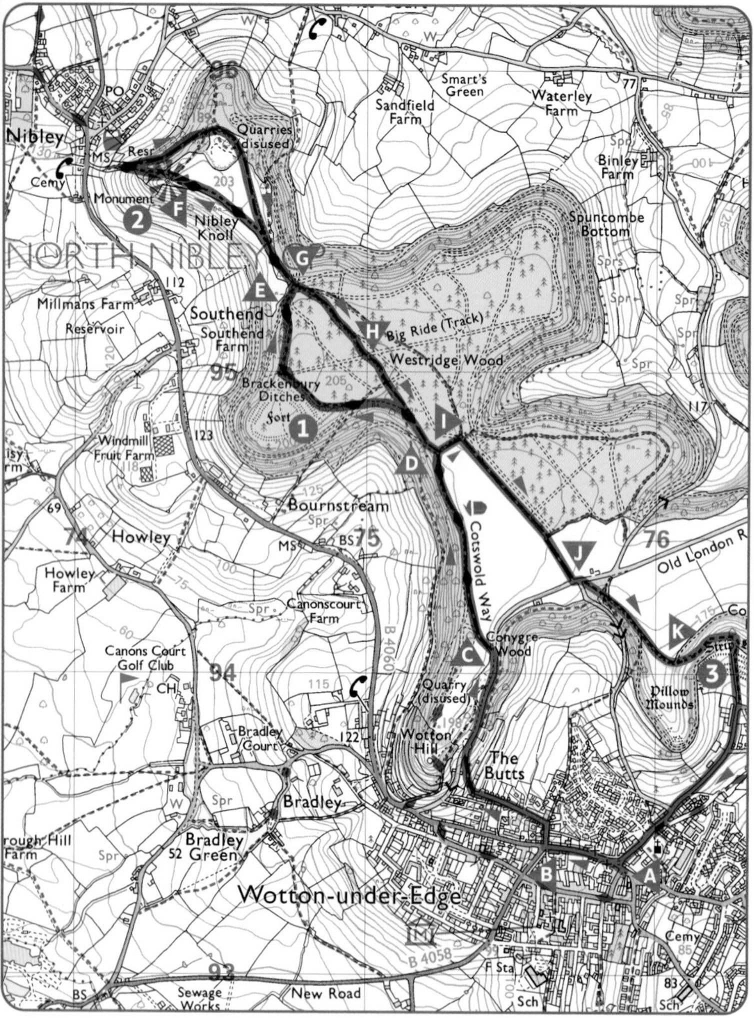
Nibley
PO
MS
Resr
Cemy
Monument
Quarries (disused)
203
Nibley Knoll
NORTH NIBLEY
112
Millmans Farm
Reservoir
Southend
Southend Farm
Big Ride (Track)
Westridge Wood
Brackenbury Ditches
Fort
205
123
Windmill Fruit Farm
Smart's Green
Sandfield Farm
Waterley Farm
Binley Farm
Spuncombe Bottom
Bournstream
Howley
Howley Farm
MS
BS
Old London R
Cotswold Way
Canonscourt Farm
Canons Court Golf Club
CH
Conygre Wood
Quarry (disused)
Pillow Mounds
Bradley Court
122
Wotton Hill
The Butts
Bradley
Bradley Green
Wotton-under-Edge
B 4060
B 4058
F Sta
Cemy
Sewage Works
New Road
BS
Sch

② The monument was erected in 1866 in memory of William Tyndale, who was born near here some time between 1490 and 1495. He was greatly concerned that ordinary people should be able to follow the Bible in English so he began translating the New Testament from Latin in the early 1520s. His work and unorthodox views attracted much criticism, and he felt it wise to continue the translation abroad in Hamburg. The work was completed in 1526 and, in

Wotton-under-Edge & the Tyndale Monument

1530, he started work on the Old Testament. Despite the changing religious climate in England, the persecution continued and he was imprisoned, charged with heresy, and executed in Flanders in 1536. It is a sad irony that, just two years after Tyndale's death, Henry VIII ordered that every church in England should have an English Bible.

F Turn right on to the sunken track and climb uphill to a gate. Walk through (or past) the gate and take the left fork through the woodland. Carry on across the field, through the gate and back to the complex of tracks.

G Continue ahead to the left of the large tree to a junction. Turn left, then after a few yards fork right up a bridleway to a major track.

H Cross straight over and, at the next track, turn left along the same track used on the outward journey to the well-defined path on the left.

I Turn left and, after 100yds (90m) turn right just before the 'T' junction down the track beside the field to the road.

J Turn left, then immediately right along the path to Coombe Hill. After 100yds (90m) turn right at a track and emerge from the trees to a stile.

K Bear half-left downhill past the telegraph pole towards the trees. Pick up the path and follow it downhill across the slope down to the fence. Turn left and cross two stiles on the right. Continue down to the road and turn right back into the village.

3 These are the remains of strip lynchets – an ancient method of farming sloping land. Earth would be extracted from one edge of the terrace and deposited at the other to smooth out the contours and create areas of flatter land that could be more easily cultivated. The lynchets are of uncertain age.

The tower of the largely 15th century church is held by some to be one of the finest in the county. Inside are the famous life-size brasses of Thomas Berkeley and his wife Margaret which are thought to date from the time of Margaret's death in 1392. The organ was constructed in about 1720 and originally belonged to St Martin in the Fields, London, where it was frequently played by Handel. The church acquired it in 1800 when it was put up for sale.

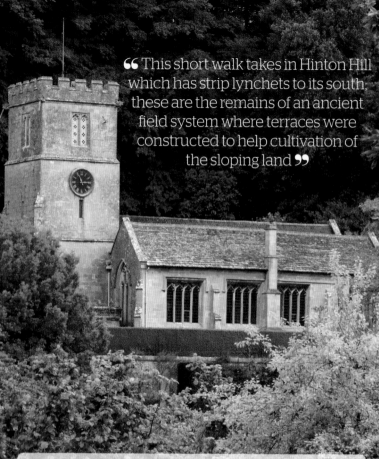

66 This short walk takes in Hinton Hill which has strip lynchets to its south; these are the remains of an ancient field system where terraces were constructed to help cultivation of the sloping land 99

This may be only a short walk but it is rich in history. Dyrham is a small village, clustered around the church and walled grounds of the mansion of Dyrham Park. The 13th century Church of St Peter is nestled against the side of a wooded hill. Inside is a Norman font, and a brass of Sir Morys Russell and his wife which is at least 400 years old.

The historical importance of Hinton Hill is much greater than the hillfort and lynchets suggest. As you walk past the hill or stand in the fort, you can almost visualize the British struggling uphill against the Saxons on the hilltop, culminating in a battle with a significant outcome for Saxon settlement in Britain.

Dyrham & Hinton Hill

Dyrham Park

DISTANCE: 2¼ miles (3.5 km)

TIME: 1¼ hours

START/END: ST737756 Dyrham

TERRAIN: Easy; (some mud)

MAPS:
OS Explorer 155;
OS Landranger 172

Route instructions

A Park in Dyrham and walk uphill to the small green. Turn left signed 'St Peter's Church' and 'Cotswold Way', past Dyrham House to the Cotswold Way bridleway on the right.

1 Dyrham Park was originally an ancient enclosure for deer. The current house stands on the site of a former Tudor manor, rebuilt at the end of the 17th century by William Blathwayt, then Secretary of State. In the late 18th century the formal gardens were cleared and replaced with landscaped parkland under the direction of Humphrey Repton. The house and deer park now belong to the National Trust.

B Turn right and walk uphill passing through the metal gate. Follow the path alongside the wall to a 'public footpath' sign just before the road.

2 These low banks are the remains of an ancient field system of strip lynchets, probably medieval in age. The terraces eased cultivation by creating areas of flatter land in otherwise sloping ground. The land here has been farmed since prehistoric times and local finds have included flint tools.

C Turn left following the direction of the sign down to a stile where several hedges meet.

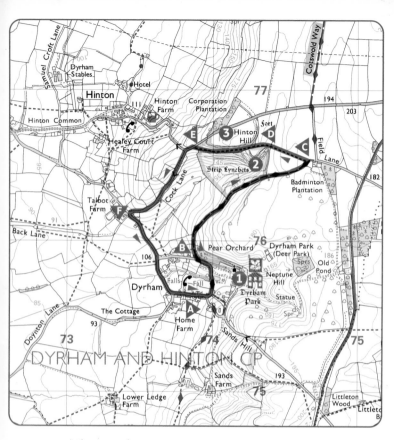

Cross the stile and continue uphill to the right of the hedge. Walk past the hillfort, on either the higher or lower path, down to the road.

3 Hinton Hill is the site of the AD577 Battle of Deorham, scene of a Saxon victory over Celts and Britons. By occupying the hillfort and defeating three British kings the Saxons thereby captured Gloucester, Cirencester, and Bath and opened up the way for Saxon settlement further west, pushing the British into Wales and Cornwall.

Turn left at the road and after 50yds (46m) turn left again following the road downhill to the next road junction.

Turn left and pass the waterfall to take the second left turn back to the car.

94 **Short Walks in** The Cotswolds

Dyrham & Hinton Hill

Waterfall near Dyrham

Photo credits